Rain on Cabrillo

A Poetry Collection

By Mark Tulin

Copyright© 2021 Mark Tulin
ISBN: 978-93-90601-06-6

First Edition: 2021
Rs. 200/-

Cyberwit.net
HIG 45 Kaushambi Kunj, Kalindipuram
Allahabad - 211011 (U.P.) India
http://www.cyberwit.net
Tel: +(91) 9415091004
E-mail: info@cyberwit.net

Printed at Repro India Limited.

"Many of these poems take place on the California beaches of Santa Barbara and Ventura during the morning hours. My impressions reflect the energy I feel walking along the coastline, the people I notice, and the objects stuck in sand. The sea is a glorious place to let your mind wander, and to be truly humbled by its beauty."

— Mark Tulin

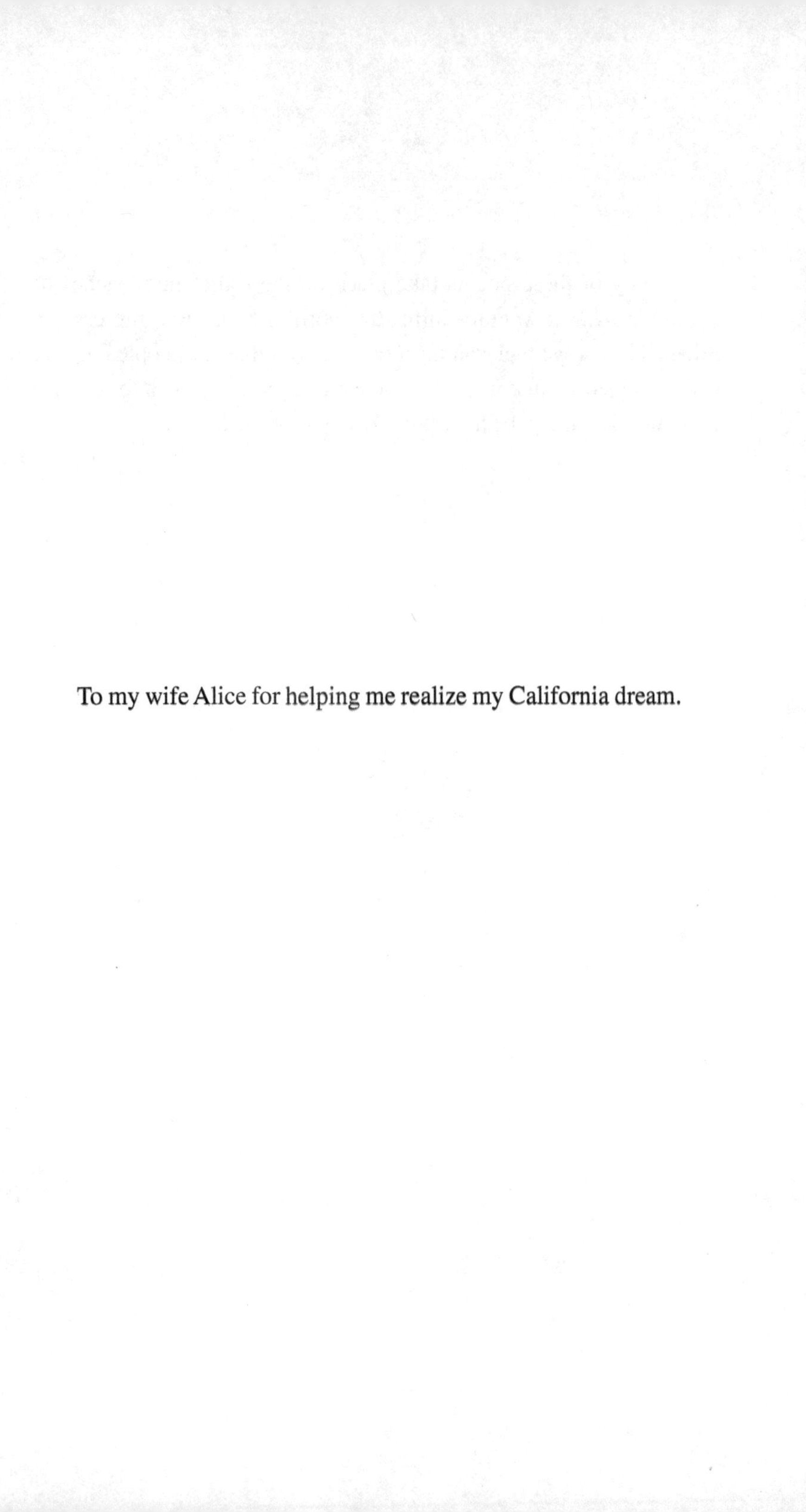

To my wife Alice for helping me realize my California dream.

Contents

Egret Sunrise

In the sea of champions,
surrounded by sandpipers,
seals, and dolphins,
I search for breakfast,
fishing on one leg,
balancing on the other,
anticipating delicious morsels,
waiting for a juicy catch

Caution is my manta
I take tiny steps
and look both ways
for red-tailed hawks,
crows, and vultures
who do not share
my love for peace

I am independent;
no pecking order,
only an equal divide
There are enough delicacies
to go around—
whirligigs and shrimp
washed ashore
for our benefit

A bountiful sunrise
in the briny mist,
an expansive food supply

Rain on Cabrillo

A whole universe
that's vast and open,
clawing waves breaking
in the sun's glow of morning.

Yoga Nature

I do yoga in the autumn woods
Nature is my teacher
The sky is my Om
The soil of the ground, my mat
that I lengthen in an upward bend
The tree is my pose
that stables my balance
The black slate is my plank
when I feel weak and unsure
The leaves crackle under my feet
as I reverse my warrior
I skim the stones of mindfulness
across the shallow creek
of glistening waters
I breathe in the scent of pine and maple
with *ujjayi* breath
I stretch and unwind
under an emerald-blue waterfall
to loosen the tightness
of my grip.

The Hopeful Mind

It's the hopeful mind,
I'm trying to find
The one that doesn't slip
through my fingers
or fade with change,
but stays in place
during trying times

I'm not looking for anything
special or fancy
to celebrate a good fortune,
nor the serious kind
that weighs a person down

A flickering light would be fine,
an optimistic sign,
a slight bend in the road
that says something positive
is not far away

I want a little hope,
a gift of promise,
a chance to find,
a gentle tap on the shoulder
in the comfort of an easy chair.

Life's Ordinary Beauty

They say if you touch the petal
of a flower,
it heats your soul
It makes the sparrows of imagination
hover around you
You'll become tireless
in your appreciation of the world
while everyone else
grows weary
Your heart will flutter
to the subtle magic of a poem,
your voice will sing
once forgotten melodies
You'll be curious
about the simple
and make the difficult easy
So interesting
does life become,
you'll want to see
its ordinary beauty
over again.

The Crown of a Yurt

Looking out the crown
of a yurt,
I can see the hawk
circling above
and hear the energy
of the howling wolf
I can see my murky dreams
in the distance become clear
I can feel the spirit
hover beside me
As I look out the crown of a yurt,
I know I'm a part of all things
that nature has created
I know I'm not alone,
no matter where I go,
or who I've been
I can feel the soothing drumbeat
surround me,
the blueness of the Navajo sky,
the whispering winds of my ancestors
that gently guide me
Looking out the crown of a yurt,
I can feel my life change and flow
I can see my body gracefully age
with wrinkled brown skin
and the beauty of ancient wisdom.

Spinal Cloud

I form my clouds
like a child
using an Etch A Sketch
of innocence and curiosity

My magical mind
draws the clouds in the sky
with the tips of my fingers
and the voice of primal souls
I build my clouds
until it forms a spine
that extends high
above the celestial body
Like a deity,
I arrange my clouds
in a fluffy dream,
seeing the world
from inside out,
reflecting its miracles.

Raindrops

always loved
when it rained
to look out the window
from an angled view
in the sea of coffee
with sleepy eyes
in a shadowy room
where it's just me
and the sound
of raindrops
tapping.

Mountain View

It was not the search for enlightenment
in the foggy Santa Ynez mountains
It wasn't the beauty of a panoramic view
It was the solitude
that nurtured my soul
The peace in my steps
on the dusty trail floor
I was quietly listening
for the color of my hopes,
the vision in my heart
I was deciding my future
in the landscape of unspoken words.

Rock of Morro Bay

The looming big rock of Morro Bay
peeks from the comforting fog
She welcomes all forms of life,
guards the vulnerable
and the lost
Harboring the seals, birds
and the otters,
directs the captain's journey
around the anchored ships,
the shoddy piers,
sirens with alluring voices
and the sunken chests
not yet found
In her misty midday glory
peering from the haze,
horns of seafaring vessels
announce the coming of
the sun.

Walking in Sand

I slowly walk
in changing
textures of sand

during low
and high tide
puncturing holes
in the damp earth
with each step

My bare feet land
at various angles
on both ends
of the beach
with each wave
that breaks and recedes
in each moment
I feel free.

Pallbearers

The pallbearers,
so gracious
in their strength
They volunteer
to cover me
in a shroud of love
and protection
to carry me
by rail
lifting my spirits
above the ground
to the clouds
moving me forward
into the next
domain
where there is a singular
hum
and a white light
that shines brightly
in the peaceful universe
of adventurous souls.

Ocean Whispers

I believe in the ocean
I worship piously
in her liquid comfort without fanfare,
in her smaller bodies of saltwater,
the inlets and the bays,
along her shoreline where seaweed
skids into a foamy paste,
exchanging a few sacred whispers,
a heavenly sun to illuminate her presence,
an impromptu hymn from the saints
to commemorate her lasting grace
and a succession of minor miracles
that pass slowly from one wave to the next.

A Drifting Halo

The cool of the ocean
and the warmth of the heavens
come together
to form a slow-moving halo
that lingers in the misty atmosphere

A welcoming celestial sheath
that grazes over the boats below,
and continues its journey
crossing mountaintops
of green and gold

And when the hot sun appears
in the early afternoon
over a jagged Pacific coast,
the sunlight transforms this drifting halo
into a sky of Rembrandt blue.

Heart-Shaped Shell

I'll find you a heart-shaped shell,
put it to your ear, and you can listen
to the rush of my breath
With each pulsing wave,
we'll get closer
The bigger the curl,
the louder the echo

I'll take you out
past the surf,
past the buoy
that nods its head
to lift us up
We'll paddle out to sea
and together we'll float
in the rhythm and dance
of our shining devotion.

Island of Solace

My mind is reborn near Jamaica
on an uninhabited island
It never gets above eighty degrees
and rarely below sixty
It has a perfect Caribbean landscape
with fresh fruit and vegetables
The ocean is turquoise, the sky, Olympic blue

My mind is an island of solace,
drifting in a quiet sea
Alone, I spend my time to heal,
a love-marooned castaway,
drinking coconut water from a straw,
dining on salmon and grilled snapper
by a campfire under a blue moon.

A Spring Moment

I often remind myself
how much I love the first day of spring
It appears unexpectedly
when the world seems cold
and imperfect,
when my youthful soul yearns
for a blooming flower
in one fragrant moment

The sun doesn't have to shine
The world doesn't have to feel safe or stable
Nothing has to be in order
or to make sense
It is the first day of my favorite season
when I feel most grateful
to be a small part of a grand universe,
that gave me my first breath.

Catching a Glimpse

Multitasking and running on autopilot,
my mind gets caught between gears
Up a snowy incline, down a slick road,
bubble gum stuck to my soles
Sometimes I lose track
of the years that just passed,
muted by life's frantic pace,
moments that race by like speeding trains
But when I take time to fully open my eyes,
I catch a glimpse of nature's mercy,
feel the rush of an ocean breeze,
floating with the moving cloud.

Growing Together

We are both flowers on a summer day
Growing together
Absorbing the effervescent sun
Birds drifting in levitation
Souls rooted in a field of green
Our delicate petals opening, curving
Expanding outward with the universe
Bees buzzing innocently around us
Hummingbirds drinking our nectar
All of nature approving of us
We are in harmony with the earth
Celebrating our love in the morning
Amidst the reds, purples, and golds.

Light of an Early Sun

I surf upon the blue water
with the light of an early sun
and hear the sounds of the ocean
like a soothing metronome

I peer into the distance
paddling with cupped hands
heading toward the horizon
drifting with the fog

I feel the misty refreshing cool
in a buoyant swell of mercy
in a strong wave of energy
wrapped in a spongy suit of glory.

Patch of Grass

I hear the world
from a patch of grass
on the courthouse lawn
With my ear to the earth,
I hear a vibration from a distant quake,
the tires of screeching cars,
clock-hands spinning,
and boot heels on the cement
I hear a bicycle ride by,
a skinny youth on a banana seat,
the rush of a whispering wind,
the glow of a smiling moon,
the hot sun in the Caribbean,
the ocean tide rolling in and out,
and my blood pulsing through
the universe.

Crow on the Lamppost

Crow resting on the lamppost,
while there's still some daylight,
knowing that all too soon,
he'll fly effortlessly
down the winding seaside road,
floating easily into the salty air
through lush foliage and palm trees,
past beach houses and tourists on bicycles,
over creaky boardwalks and dunes,
near little children with buckets and shovels
to the edge of the sea.

Gentle Waves

Gentle waves today,
don't have to push too hard,
can take a moment
to breathe in a slow breath
as leisurely as the sun rises,
as sleepy as the Channel Islands
slumber in the distance

I can float on my board
and not worry about
catching a wave,
and daydream
here in the easy life
where time moves at a crawl,
and we never grow old.

A Sacred Migration

They arrived from a larvae dimension,
blew past me in a magical blur,
whirling in steadfast discipline,
a zillion yellow, black, and white
migrating butterflies
fluttering in syncopated rhythms
A series of rapid wing movements
while everything else stood still

As the Monarchs migrated south,
nothing got in their way
Not the tall buildings or the oak trees,
or even the dark mysteries crossing the sea
They were on a sacred mission
to find a warmer place to reside,
to ease their population flow,
and to see the holiest of holy in Mexico.

A Swirling Van Gogh Sky

I wake up to an epiphany
An April morning of solemnity
An ocean flowing with passion
A swirling Van Gogh sky
A burning masterpiece
Of light and color
Radiant in its bounty
Rotating on the earth's axial tilt
A spinning kaleidoscopic globe
Orangey reds and mystical blues
Awakening dormant lives.

Monet on the Bridge

I imagine Monet
setting up his easel
on the wooden bridge
that I walk across every day

It overlooks the stone creek
that tunnels through the trees,
and thorny succulents
warmed by the yellow sun

Monet could have painted
its light and shadow
and the waterless stream
that used to flow so effortlessly

Now a bed of rocks and bones,
of stories never told,
and people whose pastel-colored
lives washed away

Monet would have seen
the hidden silhouettes
in mauve and gold,
sap dripping off the branches
of Eucalyptus trees.

Rain on Cabrillo

I pull over on Cabrillo
to watch the rain
through my car window,
a blur of swaying palm trees
and cloud-burst windy skies,
an impression by chance,
an engraving on a wet afternoon
into a waterfall of glory
Pouring rain, a haze of simplicity,
subdued and opulent,
channeling liquid energy
into one narrow moment
of youth and purity.

De La Vina Street

I like walking in a straight line
or a zigzag
across De La Vina Street,
past parks with bright flowers,
and circle the large oaks
and Eucalyptus trees

I enjoy its wide avenue
with swaying palms,
a warming sun, a mandolin playing,
and the scent of lavender
wafting in the ocean breeze

I like to hear bluebirds chirping,
see the sparrows splashing
in a marble birdbath,
and watch the gulls soar in single file
like jet fighters overhead

I like to walk mindfully,
noticing my breath,
the length of my step,
and how my hip feels
with each rotation

Down the street,
past Spanish-style homes,
creameries with shakes and splits,
taquerias with bean burritos,
silver-coated Labradors on studded leashes
and purring cats on windowsills.

Calla Lilies

She paints in a quiet corner
of a coffeehouse,
destined to dip her brush
into a small tub of water,
and dab it into an array of pastels
onto a small white canvas
and paint Calla lilies
in watercolor

She paints in gentle strokes,
taking her time around curves,
like a woman's figure,
long green stems,
a yellow center,
moon-colored petals
ready to flower
by soft, knowing hands.

It's Cleansing Time

After the storm,
a tugboat
tows the barge to our cove,
a long-legged structure,
with a crane that
reaches up like a creature
from the sea

The barge's wide hoses
float with crystal sunlight,
invading our privileged lives,
pumping a congested marina
to ease the Pacific flow

It is cleansing time
for our murky water,
the barge, only a temporary
visitor, a blemish
on an otherwise
perfect seascape

It is a moment of necessity,
to free our boats
stuck in the harbor,
people's dreams
tied to a dock,
their hopes full of mud

In order to protect
our maritime space,
there has to be maintenance,
where the sunset meets the dawn,
and the outboard motors
create a soothing sound.

Ninja Hero

Eluding the beach patrol,
the wild man brandishes a sword
of driftwood and sweat,
great and slender is his Katana
on his encampment by the dunes

He spins with one hand,
switching to the other,
enchanting the universe
with his spirit to defend
and sacrifice his life for another

He is a stealth disrupter
with a raccoon tail,
a wiry-haired recluse
with a courageous soul,
turbulent like the sea

He cultivates his art daily,
honoring his ninja ancestors
and his guides, the wind and sun
Camouflaged in deception,
he lives by the nomadic code.

Kayaking at Sunrise

I paddle at sunrise
between emptiness
and the hymn of seabirds,
sailing of pelicans
in life's nascent state

I get immunity on the waters,
gliding across at daybreak,
a peaceful foray of privacy,
alone with the saints,
communing with the goddesses

I disconnect from the world
of human chatter,
words that don't matter,
digital and computerized devices,
and the drone of TV

Before I leave to work,
I breathe in the cool air,
relax in my cozy marina,
grateful for its luxury
More valuable than gold

I develop a tempo on the kayak,
moving with grace and agility
I navigate through eternity,
encircling the blue-green sphere,
and conspiring with the tide

Rain on Cabrillo

I find meaning in maritime energy,
in my ocean of meditation,
finding balance
in the concentric ripples,
my freedom expands.

A California Birdbath

I envy the birds
in my neighbor's birdbath
I see the blue jays
and the finches
in their private spa

A fountain of splashes,
wings flapping,
hummingbirds sipping,
doves cooing,
a family of quails in harmony

with little worry of predators
crashing their party,
under a sheltering palm,
sun-dried feathers,
robins in adagio

I'm in a birdwatching trance,
imagining faraway skies
California dreaming,
alongside a concrete Aphrodite,
surrounded by sunflowers
and Painted Ladies.

Throw and Chase

I keep tossing the red ball
into the tumbling waves,
and my dog retrieves
and his paws keep paddling
while time slows,
and we never seem to tire,
but keep our game going
in an endless succession

Throw and chase is our ritual,
a man-dog brotherhood,
our way of staying connected,
sharing the sun-splattered instant
when the morning feels fresh forever,
and the waves never cease

As the seasons pass,
we eventually grow old,
my dog will develop a bad hip
I will inherit my mother's cataracts
and my eyes too blurry
to play in the bright sunshine
on the damp sands of the beach

We will become two aging comrades
who prefer the quiet of a living room
I will lean back in my lounger,
my dog curled up by my feet
on a throw rug near a space heater,

while we nostalgically remember
my dog so excited by the chase,
and me, more than happy to throw.

The Jump

I see the prism of the universe
from my place atop the cliff
My eyes grow wide in anticipation
as I take hold of this shining moment,
when breath and heartbeat suspended,
fear and judgment gone

I stand straight with arms to the sky
and take one final breath of air,
diving deep into the boundless,
into an all-encompassing spirit,
where the beginning meets the end
and my glory christens the sea.

Ocean Analyst

I talk to the moving
ocean
as if she were my analyst
easing over
my denial
cleansing my hang-ups
and my relationship
confusion

The ocean
sees right through me
and knows me better
than myself,
absorbs me in her
morning mist
and the deepest mysteries
of my dark.

Abiding Minds

At the edge of the jetty,
I rest on a flat rock
with shivering bones
and eyes that water

Like a resting bird,
I sit in peace
while the sea around me
speaks in windblown words
and broken sails,
ships beached and capsized

On a tide of choppy energy,
nature takes many strange turns,
eluding peace, expanding space
before the universe wakes
from its nightmare

Only pelicans fly in a straight line,
abiding minds gliding,
skimming the shimmery surface,
those teachers of the sea
with a marvelous intuition,
they grasp more of life's lessons.

Hungry Refugee

Sometimes I feel like a refugee
with a yellow stripe,
walking along the coastline,
searching with my sidekick
sifting and digging
through the sand,
diving into trash
that blew along the dune

There are things
I don't know,
and don't care to understand
My life satisfies on chance,
feeling the push and pull
of my natural selection
as I scour the beach
on instinct.

Postcard from Ventura Beach

Sound
light
rolling waves
sky rising high
and outward
the music
played by nature
without human melody
restful
in its peace
nothingness
in thought
blissful
eyes seeing
eternity
sand and water
birds flying
fish swimming
quietly reaching
nirvana.

Bonfire

We light this fire
with planks of driftwood
on cool Ventura nights
hearing the ocean roar

Like our youthful passion
that will never fizzle out,
a desire that will last
for an eternity

Another log onto the fire,
to build up our spirits,
to purify our bodies
with the smoke of our destiny

The bonfire lights up the sky
with resurrecting fire,
turning old ideas
into hopeful beginnings.

Dangle from the Moon

Between tall palms
where the sky opens up,
I see past the earth
into an unlimited realm

I can understand
the way of all things,
find my place in
the universe

Between tall palms,
I can dangle from the crescent moon
with one hand, and catch stars
with the other

I can dream up a fantasy
that might come true one day,
launch my own rocket ship
without being called a fool

I can hang out with Venus,
float around the solar system,
avoiding asteroids in space
like a boundless schoolyard game.

August Breath

On the cement of my city sidewalk,
I avoided stepping on the cracks
as I skipped to the schoolyard
to play ball games with my friends

I lacked the confidence
of my older brother
who believed that he led
a remarkable life

He wanted to teach me his secrets,
but I waited for the sun,
the blooming of summer flowers
and running around imaginary bases

It was the sweet August breath
and not my older brother
that made me feel good inside,
like the summer's first ice cream.

The Music of You

If your music could talk,
it would speak to me
about your dreams,
the childhood songs
of pink lemonade and
yellow and orange daffodils,
the moment your starry eyes
saw that curly-haired kid in overalls

Your songs would tell me
about the laughter
in your house,
the stories
your uncles shared,
the fresh empanadas
from the oven,
Granny doing cartwheels
and splits on the dance floor

All those 45s and LPs
spinning on your Magnavox,
heartthrobs strumming
Spanish guitars,
Elvis and Jerry Lee
at the sock hops rocking

I hear your music
sweet and clear,
coming through

your bedroom window
from the squeezebox man
to the doves serenading you

Music playing all day
in and around your head,
the rhythm of the rustling palm trees,
the melody of the whispering Santa Paula winds,
static at times on the AM radio,
but your vinyl never skipped a beat.

Daybreak Rises

On the West Coast,
stars hang over
palm trees,
crescent moons
display a gentle tilt,
nights grow shorter,
tides move further
out to sea,

daybreak rises,
setting up its stakes,
like the homeless
who line the dunes
with makeshift tents,
who fish for food
and bury their past
deep in the sand.

Flower Power

I walk in beautiful gardens
to feel the flower power,
to ride its pollen grains
to plants unknown,
to fly with the wind
and rest in green meadows
where the roses cluster,
to dream of my first yearning
where memories were sweet,
and love bloomed,
and wilted.

Truth's Slippery Essence

As a poet,
I search for faith,
speak to what's real
but I seldom do
Instead, I become one man
with two minds
and notions crossed

It's not easy
being a sojourner
of righteousness
It's downright hard
to be a rebel of honesty
when there's a revolution
of one

I reach out with good intentions
and grab truth's slippery essence
with uncertain fingers
and watch my version of reality
slide from my grasp
into murky waters.

South End Tacos

Here the line never ends
There's always a laidback dude
in a pair of flip-flops
reading the menu
like the Tao Te Ching

There's always a hot girl in daisy dukes
who could never decide,
while her muscular boyfriend
buys a box-full of shrimp tacos,
heavy on the pico de gallo

There's always a faint smell
of hashish in the air
coming from a parked car
with glassy-eyed teenagers
seeing the world in Rubik's cubes

Next door at the batting cage,
a little kid always swings and misses,
or pops a foul into the net,
like his only chronic regret
at a pitching-speed of 30 mph

A train always passes, tooting its horn,
past the South End Taco truck
with the smell of fresh carnitas,
and a Mexican guy cleaning the tables,
with a rag he's used since last December

Rain on Cabrillo

There's always a hippy bus
in a psychedelic rainbow of colors,
parked illegally by the loading zone,
full of tie-dye girls with munchies,
singing Grateful Dead songs.

A Wandering Goat by the Sea

The kid follows a sandy trail
by the ocean's edge
Surprises the canines
and their owners
with his hooves, small tail
and pointed head

Cross-eyed
and goateed,
he is an alien
in the new world,
once raised for his milk, meat, and skin
now an adorable pet
for the upwardly mobile set

The pet goat can only bleat,
make a nagging plea
and complain about his strange
domestic life by the sea,
searching for his elusive herd,
that's nowhere in sight

He yearns for a partner in crime,
a friend to jump over rocks,
tear up a fence,
eat a vegetable garden,
or graze the sloping hills,
creating havoc in the countryside.

Cubist Unity

When I walk into a non-denominational
church, I see the many colors of smiling faces,
and the talents of men and women
I soon realize that we are all one
in a Cubist unity, pieces of the same puzzle,
although not in their perfect place

While some have smooth edges,
others are a jagged collection of souls,
people with slightly different angles—
A pretty face, a strong, helping hand,
and a congregation who'd never abandon you
in the dark

We are indistinguishable,
part of the same planet of people,
needing to light candles,
wanting to share in prayer,
and washed clean by the water.

Tearful Tsunami

A torrential downpour
washed away her dreams,
and took her down
a spiral of despair

I rushed toward her
like a lifeguard,
rescuing the rain-soaked girl,
whose broken spirit
left her drowning
in a tearful tsunami

I found her in dangerous waters,
gave her a life preserver
to hold,
a shoulder
to cry on,
and a heart
that would never break.

A Prideful Glide

Drifting on fumes
from family and friends,
we glide over the Pacific,
over sailing ships and jetties,
flapping in syncopated rhythms
of pelicans undulating

We swoop and soar,
catching each other's backdraught,
having faith in our leader
who guides us by instinct

We take a prideful glide into splendor,
making new pathways in the air.

Atop a Speeding Bullet

To catch the big one
To be brave enough
 to ride an unpredictable wave
 and to balance on its apex

To watch the world
atop a speeding bullet
To know the power in its curl
that lasts as long as a carnival ride

And then to allow yourself
to be eaten and broken,
and to casually get back
on your polyurethane board.

Reflection of My Inner Self

I looked at my yoga mat,
the one I worshipped for ten years,
and could see a reflection of my inner self

I saw much struggle and anxiety,
the daily imbalance and insecurity

I felt the neurotic energy of my collective conscious
on the molded rubber atop a hardwood floor,
and realized how much I strive to live forever

If only I could let go of mortality
If only I could enjoy life's
sweet catastrophe.

Cryptic Bloom

In knotty, tangled trees, I grow
yellow and red
in a bed of soft grass,
at a park in a city square

I bloom in the midst
of botanic confusion,
spreading my petals,
despite the snaking roots

I embrace what's left
of the sun,
swaying gently
to an ocean breeze
from a distant sea

I welcome visitors,
mothers with small children,
old men with walking sticks,
who haven't seen me in a year,
surprised I had bloomed again.

Upon Sunrise

Once sunrise occurs,
I shake out the sand,
and fold my blanket
I escape another night
of darkness and whispers

I store my blanket
into a traveling sack,
slip-on my tongue-less shoes
and stretch my legs
on flat ground,
raising my arms
toward the clouds

I don't know where
I'm headed,
but have a vague idea
that if I follow the signs,
I will make it to another
resting place

If I could maintain my strength,
avoid the poison that lurks
in grains of dusty air,
and spoiled food,
I will safely hide
between temporary roots,
and a false sense of security.

Acknowledgments

Vita Brevis Press: "Yoga Nature"
Luna: "Raindrops" "Gentle Waves"
Red Wolf Editions: "Walking in Sand" "Growing Together"
Amethyst Review: "Ocean Whispers" "A Sacred Migration"
Spillwords: "A Drifting Halo" "Patch of Grass" "Abiding Minds"
"The Hopeful Mind"
Free Verse Revolution: "Island of Solace"
The Drabble: "A Spring Moment"
Whispers and Echoes: "A Swirling Van Gogh Sky"
The Local Train Magazine: "Rain on Cabrillo"
Duane's PoeTree: "De La Vina Street"
Being Known: "It's Cleansing Time"
Scrittura: "Ninja Hero" "Kayaking at Sunrise"
Gardening, Birding, and Outdoor Adventure: "A California
Birdbath"
Visual Verse: "The Jump"
Flapper Press: "Ocean Analyst" "Hungry Refugee" "Postcard
from Ventura"
The Mindful Word: "Bonfire" "August Breath"
Five Willows Literary Review: "Daybreak Rises" "Flower
Power" "Truth's Slippery Essence"
The Daily Drunk: "South End Tacos"
Macrina Magazine: "Cubist Unity"
Academy Of The Heart And Mind: "Tearful Tsunami" "A
Prideful Glide" "Atop a Speeding Bullet" "Light of an Early Sun"
"Dangle from the Moon"
The Magnolia Review: "Reflection of My Inner Self"
Haight Ashbury Literary Journal: "Cryptic Bloom"
As Above So Below Issue 6: "Upon Sunrise"